This book belongs to

_____

This book is dedicated to my children - Mikey, Kobe, and Jojo.

Copyright © 2024 Grow Grit Press LLC. All rights reserved. No part of this book may be reproduced in any form without permission in writing from the publisher. Please send bulk order requests to info@ninjalifehacks.tv

Paperback ISBN: 979-8-89614-021-4
Hardcover ISBN: 979-8-89614-023-8
eBook ISBN: 979-8-89614-022-1

Printed and bound in the USA.
NinjaLifeHacks.tv

Ninja Life Hacks®
by Mary Nhin

During a game, if we both want the same toy, I might feel frustrated, but I remember to stay calm and talk about it.

I even help my friends agree on what to play by finding a solution that makes everyone happy. This is called a win-win solution. It might be hard at first, but it's always worth it.

I haven't always been so good at finding solutions. I used to feel really upset when we couldn't agree. I'd either give up or feel bad that things didn't go my way.

T: Take – Take a deep breath.
A: Ask – Ask questions to understand the other person's perspective.
L: Listen – Listen carefully to what they say and how they feel.
K: Keep calm – Stay calm and friendly as you find a win-win solution.

This hack can help you **T.A.L.K.** your way through any negotiation!

The next day, I decided to try something new. When my friend and I disagreed about which game to play, I didn't get upset. I took a deep breath and started to T.A.L.K.

At recess, we both wanted the same ball. Instead of arguing, I **asked** questions and **listened** to understand what my friend wanted. We decided to play a game that used the ball in a way we both liked.

I realized that it's okay to have different ideas and that working together can help everyone feel good. What's important is that we keep talking and listening to each other. From then on, I didn't feel like Negotiator Ninja was such a tough role to play. I noticed that I could help us all have more fun by using T.A.L.K.

We're getting better at TALKing!

T.A.L.K.

Check out the fun Negotiator Ninja lesson plans at ninjalifehacks.tv

I love to hear from my readers. Email me your feedback or thoughts on what my next story should be at info@ninjalifehacks.tv   Yours truly, Mary

 @marynhin @GrowGrit #NinjaLifeHacks

 Mary Nhin   Ninja Life Hacks

 Ninja Life Hacks

 @officialninjalifehacks

www.ingramcontent.com/pod-product-compliance
Lightning Source LLC
LaVergne TN
LVHW070436070526
838199LV00015B/526